# The Art
## of
# Painting
## on
# Silk

*Also in this series*

The Art of Painting on Silk Volume 2 – Soft Furnishings

# The Art of Painting on Silk

## Volume 1

Translated by **Gisela Banbury**
Edited by **Pam Dawson**

SEARCH PRESS

First published in Great Britain 1987
Search Press Ltd
Wellwood, North Farm Road
Tunbridge Wells, Kent TN2 3DR

Reprinted 1988

Translated by Gisela Banbury and based on the
following books published by Christophorus-Verlag,
Freiburg im Breisgau:

1. *Aparte Seidenmalerei* by Christel Keller (Brunnen-Reihe 208)
2. *Seidentüecher handbemalt* by Friederike Franzkowiak (Brunnen-Reihe 234)
3. *Seidenkissen und -bilder handbemalt* by Rosemarie Kindervater (Brunnen-Reihe 239)
4. *Seide, Farbe . . . und was man daraus machen kann* by Christel Keller (Hobby & Werken)
5. *Bemalte Seide: Kleidung und Accessoires* by Karen Coussa (Hobby & Werken)
6. *Seidenmalerei in Aquarelltechnik* by Hedwig Danner (Brunnen-Reihe 245)
7. *Seidenmalerei: Schmuck, Bilder, Kleidung* by Christiane Köehl (Brunnen-Reihe 248)
8. *Variable Seidenmal – Motive* by Catherine Grotemeyer (vorlagenmappe)

Copyright © Christophorus-Verlag GmbH, Freiburg im Breisgau,
respectively 1982, 1985, 1985, 1984, 1985.

English Edition copyright © Search Press Limited 1987

This edition distributed in the United States of
America by Arthur Schwartz & Co, 420 East 82nd
Street, New York, NY 10028.

Photographic credits: Ulrike Schneiders (1, 2, 3, 5, 6, 7) Christian Kaminski (4) and Rainer Meier-Wittmar (4); Drawings and diagrams by Christel Keller, (1); Lajos Jobbagy (1, 57); Friederieke Franzkowiak (2); Rosemarie Kindervater (3); Karen Coussa (5); drawings by Catherine Grotemeyer (8).

ISBN 0 85532 597 6

Typeset by Pentacor Ltd., High Wycombe, Bucks
Printed in Spain by A. G. Elkar, S. Coop. Bilbao 12

# CONTENTS

# Introduction

It is the silkworm, a species of caterpillar or moth, which produces that most noble of textile fibres—silk. It feeds on mulberry leaves and spins itself a cocoon which can be made up of thread as much as 3,000 metres or nearly 10,000 feet in length—very fine, elastic, and strong.

Silkworms have been kept in China for over 4,000 years. The penalty for smuggling them out of the country used to be death. As a result, only the finished fabrics reached the rest of the world, along the famous 'Silk route' to Europe. In the sixth century monks are believed to have hidden the eggs of the silkworm in their staffs and smuggled them to Byzantium. Silkworms also reached India and Japan. In Italy silk was produced in the twelfth century, in France the first silk was woven in Lyons in the sixteenth century. Painting on silk, which by then was highly developed in the Far East, was now taken up widely in France, and French style and techniques came to influence the rest of the Western world. Soon, however, it became forgotten, until early in the present century when it was rediscovered in southern France and Brittany.

Nowadays even the amateur can achieve excellent results with modern silk paints. The brilliance of these silk paints and the luxuriousness of the smooth, rich silk fabrics is an irresistible combination.

Two attributes are essential for the silk artist: not simply drawing skill and colour sense, as might be expected, so much as patience and diligence. With these the basic skills of silk painting are quickly learned, for the craft is not as difficult to work as it at first appears to be.

Is it an expensive hobby? It is certainly not cheap for, of course, silk is a precious material. Nor will your first product be a masterpiece! So start by practising with small-scale items. These will quickly reveal, however, what a wealth of possibilities there is in silk painting, for no other material or technique produces such luminous colours, and such experiments can lead on to magical results.

It is beyond the scope of this book to describe all the possible variations, but in the opening section of the book the basic techniques are explained and the few basic tools and materials that are necessary are described. In the rest of the book the main emphasis is on the objects you can make—cushions, pictures, scarves, dresses, and other, smaller items.

Whether one is an experienced artist working in a studio, or a beginner painting on the kitchen-table or in the garden, it is possible to learn and to enjoy. The experienced artist will draw inspiration for his designs from the world around him; the beginner, on the other hand, will find suggestions in this book for drawings that are ideal for teaching technique. It is also best to begin with small items, such as a bag or greetings card, and then to advance from these to the more ambitious and fashionable projects which are illustrated in this book.

The drawings in the last part of the book beginning on page 81 will need to be scaled up or down to a suitable size for working. Use a photocopier or pantograph.

This striking design uses simple techniques and brilliant colours to achieve the maximum effect. The completed painting would make a suitable picture, scarf or cushion cover.

# How to begin

Once you have mastered the basic techniques, this exciting craft can be used to produce original and luxurious items at relatively low costs. Be realistic about your first attempt, however, and begin with something small enough in area and simple enough in design to guarantee successful results. As your confidence grows, you will feel able to tackle some of the more complicated designs featured in this book.

Before attempting to paint on silk it is important to understand that you will never be able to reproduce an exact replica of any illustration. Silk is a natural fibre and, much like wool, varies in quality and texture. Paints may also vary from one manufacturer to another in texture and colour. Another point to bear in mind is that an original design may have been drawn free-hand, without any clear lines of reference, so is a 'one-off'. These factors, however, are what make this craft so fascinating, as you will always produce your own unique design.

Make sure you have everything you will require to hand before beginning any project. You will need to work quickly to achieve satisfactory results and if you have to break off in the middle of an operation because you have forgotten to buy a brush fine enough to paint small areas, the whole process could be ruined.

You need not make any vast initial outlay on tools or materials. Scraps of silk can be found on most remnant counters at prices to suit all purses. Keep to a few basic colours for your first project, (see colour chart on page 11)—you can add to your range as you progress. Don't go to the expense of purchasing a frame for a small item, such as a greetings card—you may already possess an embroidery frame which makes a suitable alternative. Or if you can handle a screwdriver, it is a simple matter to make a fixed frame to any size.

## Tools

The basic tools needed for silk painting are easily obtainable in art and craft shops or by mail order from specialist suppliers. Some tools can even be made up at home. However the beginner's kit should contain the following:

1 wooden frame
Silk fabric
Silk paints in two or three colours
Brushes
Pins
Gutta, or blocking agent
Salt
Thinner and fixing agent—as recommended by the manufacturer of the range of paints used
A colour chart—helpful in deciding on a colour scheme (see page 11)

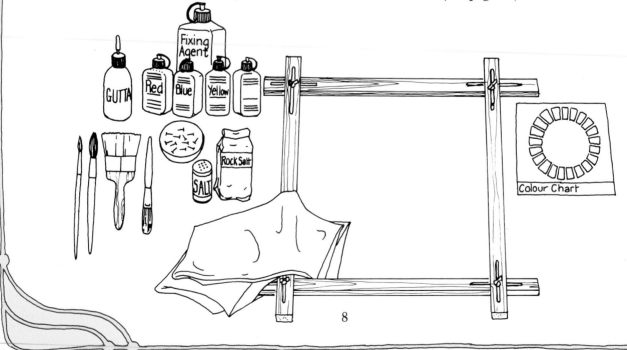

# Materials

## Frames

Silk can only be painted successfully if the fabric is evenly stretched and freely suspended. Purpose-made flat wooden frames—which can be adjusted and extended with additional pieces of wood from picture postcard size to 120in × 56in (300cm × 140cm)—are on the market (see page 9). These frames can also be readjusted during painting. For the beginner a fixed frame made from four pieces of wood screwed together with four metal angle pieces is quite sufficient; but since it is not adjustable this has to be made to the correct size of the fabric to be painted. For instance: for square scarves, which use silk 40in (100cm) wide, the inner opening should be 38in × 38in (95cm × 95cm).

Before any silk is stretched on to the frame, cover the frame with wide sellotape, so that it can be easily wiped clean with a damp cloth and no remains of paint from previous work will spoil a new piece of silk.

Small items—such as greetings cards (see page 22) may be stretched in an embroidery or Tambour frame, or placed over a jam jar or rimmed glass-dish and held in place with a strong elastic band or cord.

# Silk fabrics

There are many different silk fabrics on the market, from very shiny and transparent organza to dull, heavily textured wild silks and noil. Not all of these are suitable for every silk painting technique, indeed they will impose their own very diffent characteristics on to the design. Heavily textured silks will not, for example, take the dyes evenly. They will also tend to encourage 'bridge-building' when 'gutta' is applied (see gutta-technique, page 15)—and this will later allow the colours to break through a gutta line and run into each other. Very thick silks may need a gutta application on both sides.

For the inexperienced painter it will be best to try twill, pongé or crepe-de-chine. All these varieties are suitable for shawls and scarves. For blouses and dresses crepe-de-chine as well as georgette and silk-satin are very suitable.

Whatever type of fabric is chosen for your first project, only unbleached white, or pale cream, give backgrounds that will produce clear, brilliant colours as the paints are applied. An important point to remember is that white is a hue not represented in any range of silk paint, so the white background of the fabric is used in many designs to highlight an area, or to define outlines between blocks of colours.

As you progress in expertise, you may wish to experiment to see what effects can be obtained by using pale, pastel backgrounds. In this event, the background colour chosen will be the palest shade in a design and you will not be able to introduce any white. The background colour will also have an effect on the paints you use and it will be difficult to visualize the finished colouring of a design. For example, on a pale blue background, areas of yellow paint will produce shades of greenish-yellow.

All materials have to be washed, before they can be used for painting, in order to remove any traces of dressing and grease. Wash by hand in hand-warm water with a gentle detergent. Rinse well, roll the fabric into a towel and, when it is still damp, iron with a warm iron.

Fine silks can be torn, but thicker fabrics have to be cut carefully along the grain.

## Silk paints

Silk paints divide into two groups:
1. Alcohol-based paints, and water-based paints. Both types are marketed as a watery liquid and are applied in the same way, but thinning and fixing methods differ.
2. Water-based paints are thinned down with water to lighten their tones, and they are made permanent or 'fixed' by simply ironing the painted silk with an electric iron (see page 20).

Alcohol-based paints can also be thinned down with water, but a special thinning liquid will ensure a more even application. The fixing process is more complicated as it involves steaming (see page 20), but the end result tends to be more brilliant.

Some firms offer a brush-on fixative (see page 20). Because of the different methods of fixing and thinning it is important to read and follow carefully the manufacturer's instructions on the paint bottles. For the beginner, paints which are fixed by ironing are the easiest and cheapest to use.

Colours of the same range can be freely mixed to create new colours or different tones and shades (see opposite). Colours of different ranges or from different manufacturers should never, however, be mixed. Also it is not advisable to use gutta or fixatives of one make in combination with paints of another make. Some paints are offered in a thicker consistency. These will not run when painted on to dry silk, and they may be mixed with thinner paints of the same range.

# Simple colour mixing

Most manufacturers offer many colours in each range of silk paints, but as they can be freely mixed within each range, two or three well-chosen colours will create quite a full palette.

The colour triangle (opposite) shows the three 'primary' colours as: cadmium yellow (1) magenta (5) light blue (9).

When two of these 'primary' colours are mixed in equal quantities 'secondary' colours are created:

| | |
|---|---|
| cadmium yellow + magenta | = orange (2) |
| magenta + light blue | = violet (7) |
| light blue + cadmium yellow | = medium green (11) |

A group of six 'second-order secondary' colours is created when a 'primary' colour is mixed with a 'secondary' colour.

# Colour chart

1 cadmium yellow
2 orange
3 scarlet
4 carmine
5 magenta
6 purple
7 violet
8 ultramarine
9 light blue
10 turquoise (cyan)
11 medium-green
12 yellow-green

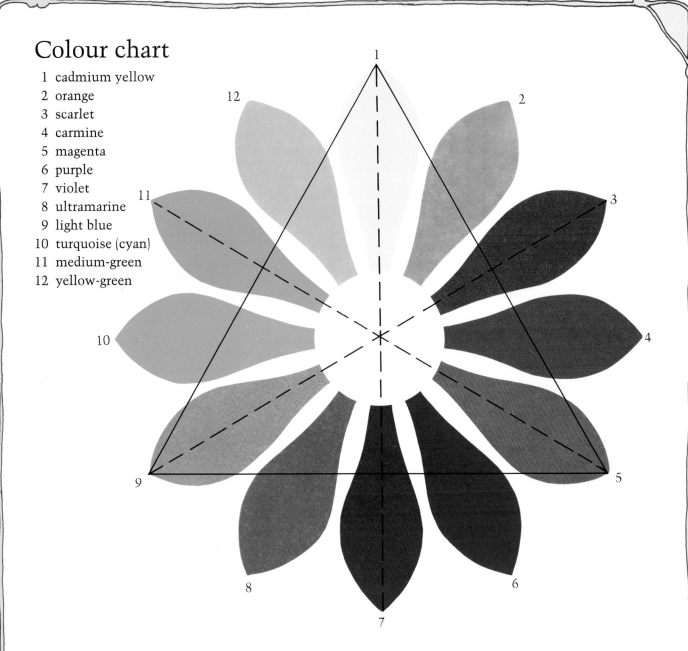

cadmium yellow + scarlet = orange (2)

scarlet + magenta = carmine (4)

magenta + violet = purple (6)

violet + light blue = ultramarine (8)

light blue + medium green = cyan (10)

medium green + cadmium yellow = yellow green (12)

The natural or white colour of the silk fabric is the lightest tone available. Any area meant to stay in the background colour is painted with a blocking agent or 'gutta' (see 'Gutta technique', page 15).

Each colour can be lightened to the gentlest pastel tones by adding more water, or a thinning agent if so recommended by the manufacturers. Black diluted will turn to greys.

**Watch point:**
When painting larger areas with mixed or thinned paint, make sure to mix enough paint, as it is not always possible to repeat a tone or colour accurately by mixing. It is better to have too much than too little. Mixed paints can be kept almost indefinitely in glass jars with well-fitting lids and preferably in the dark. Shake or stir them well before use, as the pigment sometimes settles on the bottom of the jar.

# Brushes

The most suitable brushes to use are watercolour brushes which come to a fine point. They carry a lot of paint and give it out slowly and evenly.

At the top of the range are the Japanese brushes but, for the beginner, brushes of student quality, thick, medium and fine, are quite adequate.

It is best to use one brush for each colour, so as not to contaminate their hue with any possible remaining paint of a different colour.

Brushes are not cheap and the better they are looked after the longer they will last. After use, wash them out in lukewarm water, shape them to a good straight point and keep them upside down in a glass or a jug.

Large areas of background can be painted with bunches of cotton wool or a sponge.

**Watch point:**
Either use a clothes-peg to hold the cotton wool or sponge or wear rubber gloves to protect your hands. If a fixative agent is used, it is best applied with a wide, stiff brush and by using long even strokes.

# Pins

To hold the silk fabric to the frame, stainless steel pins must be used. Map-, decor-, or drawing-pins are suitable, but there are also available in art and craft shops special three-pronged flat-headed tacks.

# Gutta, or blocking agent

A blocking agent or 'gutta' is used in the gutta-technique of silk painting (see page 15), or to block out areas of the design which the artist wants to keep in the colour of the silk fabric.

**Watch point:**
Always use the blocking agent that is recommended by the manufacturer of the range of paints you are using. Sometimes it is marketed in bottles which can be fitted with nozzles of varying sizes, sometimes the bottles themselves are pointed. There are also special gutta dispensers on offer.

The most commonly used blocking agent is transparent. When the silk is washed after the paints have been fixed, the transparent gutta will disappear and only leave a line of the original colour of the fabric, usually natural or white.

Gutta is also available in black, silver and gold. This means that the colour lines of the design drawn with gutta will remain black, silver or gold. This can look very decorative and festive, but it will not stand up to frequent washing and ironing. Dry cleaning may remove the gold and silver gutta.

**Watch point:**
Protect your ironing board with a cloth as sometimes the gold and silver will transfer itself to the board during ironing.

# Salt

To create the marbled effects of the salt technique (see page 19) special salt can be bought from silk paint suppliers, but any cooking salt can be used, fine or coarse. Salt crystals, as used in water softeners, are also suitable. Coarse salt will produce larger-scale effects, and finer salts finer marbling.

# Dressing the frame

With the frame covered with sellotape, and the silk washed and ironed as described in previous sections (page 9), we are now ready to begin.

The silk needs to be stretched evenly over the frame and as tightly as on a drum. Start at the bottom edge of the frame with the right side of the silk uppermost. Line it up with a straight edge of the fabric, and hold the silk in place with one pin or tack in each corner pulling the silk as tight as possible. Next, pin

down the centre, then the centres to the right and to the left all along the bottom edge, until the intervals are no bigger than 2in (5cm). Work in the same way along the opposite edge and finally along the two sides. Adjustable frames can now be tightened a final time.

*This shows the position of the pins, when attaching the silk to the frame.*

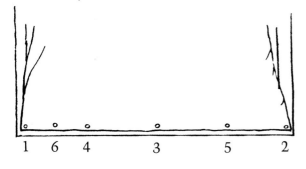

1   6   4        3        5        2

**Watch point:**
During pinning no pleats, stretch marks or wavy lines should appear on the silk fabric. To make sure that the silk is freely suspended and not anywhere in touch with the table, it is best to lift the frame off the table by supporting all four corners with four tins or small boxes. (The cardboard insides of wide sellotape rolls are ideal.)

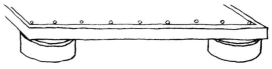

You are now ready to work in any of the following techniques: gutta, watercolour, or salt, which are described in the next chapter.

# Techniques

# Gutta technique

Gutta-technique is sometimes referred to as blocking-technique, or resist-technique, or outline-technique.

First, either sketch the design lightly on to the silk or place one of the drawings featured in this book directly behind the fabric. With fine silks the outlines ought to show through sufficiently to be copied.

Fit the gutta-bottle directly with a nozzle of suitable width or transfer the gutta to a special dispenser. Now copy the outlines of the design with gutta on to the silk and leave it to dry according to the manufacturer's instructions. This can take anything from 10–30 minutes. These gutta lines will stop the paints from running into each other. If transparent gutta is used, a line in the original colour of the silk fabric will remain. If a coloured gutta is used the line drawing will appear in the colour of the gutta used.

The designs best suited for this technique have long flowing lines without too many stops and starts, for the gutta has the tendency to start and finish with a blob.

**Watch point:**
Wipe the nozzle with a tissue before each new start.

Do not draw too slowly but with an even flow. Hold the frame against the light to check that the gutta lines are uninterrupted and have sunk into the silk properly everywhere, and make sure that all lines are closed. With very knobbly silks there is that tendency to 'bridge-building' where the gutta is trailing and not in touch with the silk. Mend any gaps and again leave it all to dry.

When the gutta is dry, the paints can be applied to the gutta-surrounded areas. Start in the middle of a 'field' with a full brush but paint only to near the edge of the 'field'. The colour will spread out to the gutta lines. Apply first the light colours of the design. Should there be a leak through an unnoticed gap in the gutta line this can be mended and covered up later with the darker colours.

Leave the painting to dry for a few hours. Next, the colours will have to be made permanent or 'fixed' according to the manufacturer's instructions (see page 20). The fixing process should also prove the colours for handwashing and dry-cleaning.

# Watercolour technique

With the watercolour technique no gutta is used to keep the colours apart; instead they are allowed to flow into each other. This technique is particularly suitable for landscapes, but the artist needs to work quickly wet on wet.

To stop the silk from drying out too quickly during painting, the whole fabric is brushed with either water or a thinner, according to the manufacturer's instructions, then paints are applied briskly on to the wet silk. Start with the lighter colours of the sky, working downwards to the medium tones of the middle distance and the darker tones of the foreground at the bottom edge of the frame.

Details can now be added by drawing some more horizontal lines on to the wet background or brushing in shapes for trees and bushes. The colours will fuse into each other with no hard lines or contours.

**Watch point:**
Start with small blots of paint, as they will spread and grow.

After the background is dry more details can be added. Brush strokes with only water or thinner will break up the even colouring, irregular watermarks will appear, and also lighter areas with darker edges and lines not unlike distant mountain ranges or softer hills.

Leave this to dry again, before adding more

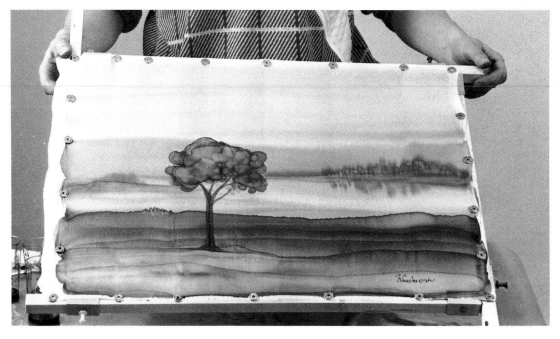

precise details like tree trunks or grasses in the foreground. Either use thickened paint, which does not run on a dry background, or use an ordinary electric hair-dryer. Hold the paintbrush in one hand, the hair-dryer, on a medium setting, in the other, and, immediately after applying the paint, blow it dry so that it has no chance to spread. If a fine brush is used some very delicate lines can be produced in good contrast to the watercolour background. A steady hand and a little practice are needed, so try it out first on some scrap material. Finally, leave everything to dry thoroughly for a few hours before fixing the colours according to manufacturer's instructions (see page 20).

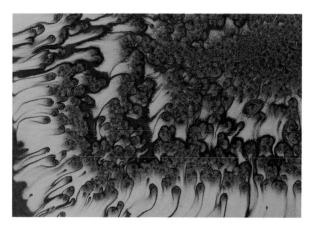

*Salt applied
before the paint
produces a
dotted pattern*

# Salt technique

Both the gutta and watercolour techniques of silk painting may be combined with each other, and either or both may be combined with the salt technique.

Since salt attracts water, if there is colour pigment suspended in the water it will be attracted by salt as well. So if kernels of ordinary salt are strewn over a damp, evenly coloured area each salt kernel will soak up the dampness from its surroundings and with it the colour pigment. The result is a marvellous, but unpredictable, marbled or clouded effect. Different salts give different patterns, so it is best to experiment.

**Watch point:**
Be careful not to have any water standing on the fabric, or the salt will 'drown'.

Leave the salt on the silk until everything is dry, then brush it off with a soft brush and fix the paints as recommended by the manufacturer (see page 20).

**Watch point:**
The dryer the salt, the quicker it will work and the more moisture it can soak up. Warm it a little in an open container in the oven before applying.

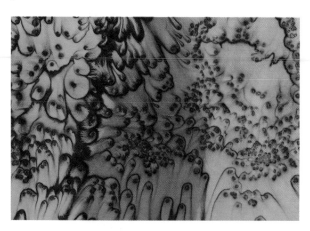

*Salt applied
to plain coloured
background using
concentrated
paint*

*Salt applied
to multi-coloured
background*

# Fixing

There are three principal ways of fixing silk paints: but whichever method you use, be sure to follow the manufacturers' instructions, and remember that you must never mix different makes of paint or fixatives.

## 1. Brushing on fixative

For some ranges manufacturers recommend a fixative in liquid form. It is brushed on after the paints are dry with a broad stiff brush. Work carefully and make sure that all of the silk fabric is well covered.

**Watch point:**
Work on a horizontal frame, otherwise some of the colours may run.

Leave to dry for one hour.
Take the fabric off the frame and handwash it in cold water. During the washing process some surplus dye may come out as well as any gutta used.
Hang up to dry; and, finally, iron. The colours should now be permanent and proved for handwashing (30°C or 86°F) and dry-cleaning.

## 2. Ironing

Some water-based paints can be fixed by simply ironing with an electric iron set to the temperature recommended by the manufacturer. After the paints are dry take the silk off the frame. Make sure that it does not touch anything wet or damp. Cover the ironing board with a clean piece of material and iron the silk all over from the 'wrong' side for 2–3 minutes. This will set the colours permanently for handwashing and dry-cleaning.

**Watch point:**
If the recommended ironing temperature is too hot for the fabric, protect it with a piece of paper between iron and fabric.

## 3. Steaming

Alcohol-based silk paints are fixed by steaming.
There are on the market purpose-built steam ovens with detailed instructions, but they are rather too expensive for a beginner.

It is possible to steam small articles, however, like scarves, shawls, pictures, cushions, or covers for lampshades, in a pressure-cooker, as follows: After the paints have dried for some hours, take the fabric off the frame and roll it very carefully into a larger piece of absorbent paper. Plain white blotting paper or wallpaper liner are ideal. The silk must lie absolutely flat, no pleats or wrinkles, and it must not overlap or touch itself. Roll the paper and silk into a sausage of about 1½in (or 4cm) diameter. Hold the roll closed with masking tape and also seal the ends. Wrap the roll loosely in aluminium foil. Semi-fold the parcel ends to allow steam to enter and to prevent condensation from running into the centre of the parcel so damaging the painted silk. Fill the pressure cooker with ¾in (2cm) of water or not quite to the base of the vegetable basket (see Fig a and b below). Fit the foil wrapped parcel into the basket without touching the sides, place the basket on the trivet inside the pressure cooker and close. Raise the pressure to 5lb per square inch and cook for about 45 minutes.
If no pressure cooker is available the steaming process can be done in a large pot with a well fitting lid, but the fixing time has to be trebled. Watch the water level – it should not be allowed to boil dry!

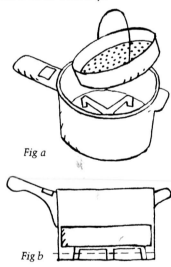

*Fig a*

*Fig b*

*A domestic pressure-cooker may be used for fixing the paints by steaming. Fig a) shows the inside of the cooker; Fig b) shows the level of the water in the bottom of the cooker and the position of the foil-wrapped silk painting.*

# Instructions for pantograph

The following pages in this book give you various designs for ideas or diagrams which you can actually copy. If you wish the design to stay the same size you can just trace it. You may, of course, wish to enlarge or reduce the actual drawings and there are several means by which you will be able to obtain an exact copy.

There are various forms of photocopiers which will enlarge or reduce on paper. There are also more sophisticated machines which will copy a design to any size, on to any material, but these can be rather costly.

The simplest way to reduce or enlarge is to use a pantograph which you can either make yourself or which you can obtain from most art and craft shops, (see Fig a). A pantograph consists of four flattened rods or pieces of wood. At the appropriate points a tracing point is fixed to these rods for tracing the lines of the original and a drawing point for making the appropriate copy. The pantograph is hinged at the crossing points which can be adjusted to enlarge or reduce the copy.

Fig a

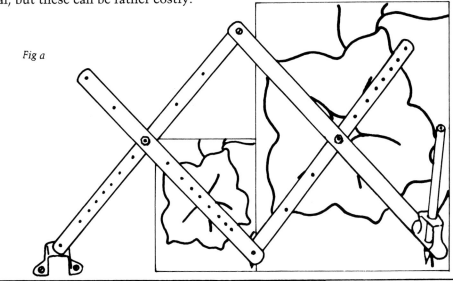

# Simple projects

If you are reluctant to test your skill at free-hand painting for your first venture, adapt one of the illustrations shown in the last section of this book. If the design is too large, choose an area which will give the effect you desire and rule this up in pencil to the size you require. For example, just one of the rose blooms shown on page 83 would make a marvellous subject for a greetings card.

For a miniature copy of a complete illustration, reduce the chart to the size you require on a photo-copier. Keep to a subject with

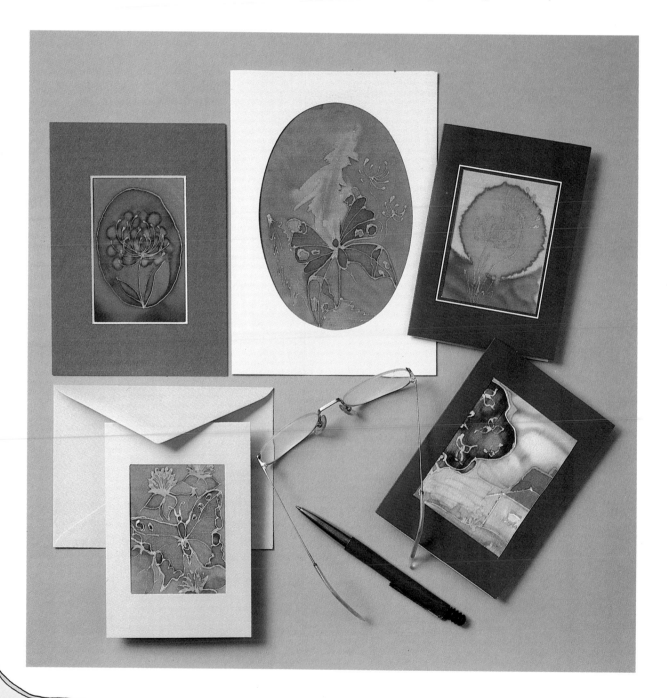

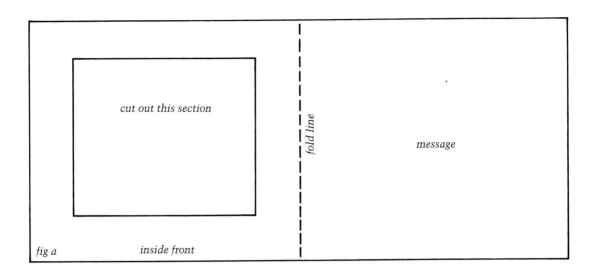

*cut out this section*

*fold line*

*message*

*fig a*　　*inside front*

clear, simple lines as once they are reduced, small areas will be difficult to paint. The illustration of the butterfly shown on page 42 would make a suitable subject for one of the small bags featured on page 24.

## Mounting a greetings card

A wide selection of ready-made mounts are available, complete with matching envelopes, but it is a simple matter to make your own mounts to any size. The card or paper you use will vary in price according to the quality and weight. Choose the colour of your mount very carefully, making sure it will enhance your silk painting. A pad of assorted coloured construction paper offers a wider variety of colours than it is possible to obtain by buying individual sheets.

You will also need sharp scissors, a ruler for trimming the card to size and some glue. Rubber solution is recommended for most gluing, as it allows the picture to be repositioned if necessary.

**Watch point:**
If you are making your own mount, before finally deciding on the size of your card make sure you can obtain an envelope to match.

Cut a rectangle from the card and fold this in half. On the left-hand side – which will be the inside front of the card – mark an area large

enough to take the silk painting, allowing about ½in (1cm) of the picture to be stuck down and leaving a margin of at least 1in (2.5cm) all round the card. Cut out this marked centre section, (Fig a).

With the right side of the silk painting facing you, lightly apply the glue as directed on the tube to the extreme edges. Place the painting face down on to the inside of the cut-out opening, making sure it is centrally positioned.

Once the glue is quite dry, fold the card in half so that the picture shows on the front and write your message on the inside.

## Greetings cards

Who would not like to receive a hand-painted greetings card? Here is an opportunity for you to use gold and silver gutta without fear. Every silk painting technique is suitable. Pre-cut mounts are available in many sizes and they will give your silk paintings a professional finish.

## Small bags or purses

Place the silk over a suitable drawing and copy the design with a soft pencil on to the silk. Frame up the silk as described on page 13 and apply gutta as indicated on page 14, following the pencil lines. Colour the small areas of the design with a fine brush, the

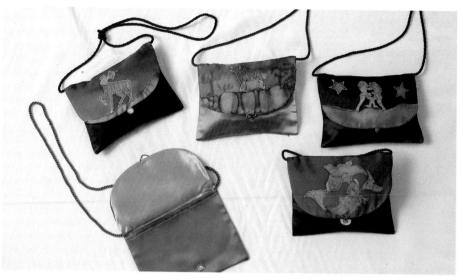

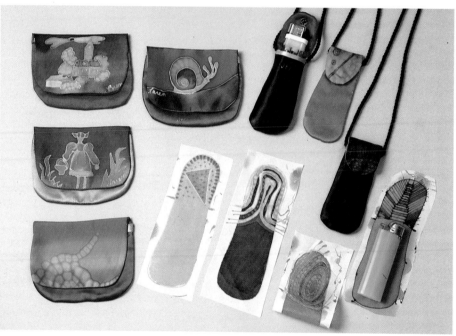

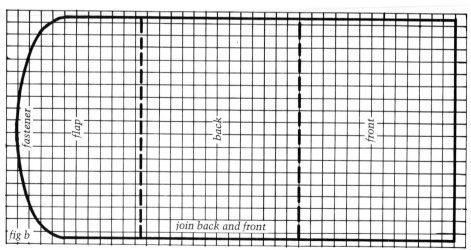

*fastener*

*flap*

*back*

*front*

join back and front

fig b

24

larger background with a large brush using large even strokes. Fix the colours as recommended by the manufacturers of the paints.

## Making a small purse

Use the pattern shown here, (Fig b), to cut out the completed silk painting and a separate piece of lining fabric. Each square on the pattern equals ¾in (2cm).

Join the side seams of the back and front on both pieces. With the wrong sides of each piece facing, insert the lining into the bag. Turn in both edges of the flap and neatly slip-stitch in place. Sew a press stud to the inside of the flap and the top of the front.

## Brooches

These small colourful items are the ideal first projects. The colour combinations may be as wild and daring as you like, and, because the designs are so small, the shaky lines of an inexperienced hand will not be obvious. Also all stops and starts of a 'gutta' line can be outside the design, so that they will not show, because they are folded around to the back.

Cover a small card disc with the silk. To give it more body, pad it with some foam rubber which is cut to the size of the cardboard disc. Fold the surplus fabric to the back. Either stick it down or sew it up. Cover the back of the brooch with another cardboard disc, which has a safety pin attached to it.

# Silk cushions

Luxurious cushions are practical yet orna-mental furnishings and need not be expen-sive. The beauty of your own original silk cushions will add the finishing touch to any room and highlight a colour scheme. Even if you are not an experienced needlewoman, cushion making presents few problems. If you can cut a straight edge and sew a plain seam, you can make a successful cushion.

First determine the size of the cushion you intend to make—18in (46cm) square is a popular size. For the cover you will need to buy sufficient silk for the painted front of the cushion and a similar amount for the plain back. As a guide, a length of 20in (51cm) from a 40in (102cm) wide fabric should be enough to cover an 18in (46cm) cushion. This will allow about 1in (2.5cm) all round for seam-ing.

Ready-made pads to fit inside the cushion cover are available in different sizes and shapes from most furnishing departments and stores. Inexpensive pads are usually filled with kapok, or a mixture of down and feathers. If you can afford to spend a little extra for a pure down ready-made pad, this will greatly enhance the softness of the silk cover.

## Making a cushion cover

Place the completed silk painting and the remaining piece of silk together, with the right sides facing each other. Tack along three of the sides of the square, about ½in (1cm) in from the edge. Insert the cushion pad very gently and check that it will fit snug-gly—if not, re-tack the seams.

Seam these three edges by machine, or by hand using small, neat back-stitches. Unpick the tacking stitches.

**Watch point:**
To give a perfect fit at the corners, the seams of the cover should now be squared off. This will ensure that there are no unsightly lumps of fabric. Before closing the remaining seam, trim each corner diagonally across, (Fig a). Take care not to cut too close to the stitches.

Turn the cover right side out and insert the cushion pad. To close the remaining opening, turn ½in (1cm) along both edges to the inside and slip-stitch them together, keeping the stitches small and neat so that they barely show.

To remove the cover for cleaning, it is an easy matter to snip through the slip-stitches and remove the pad. Once the cover has been cleaned, insert the pad and re-stitch it in position.

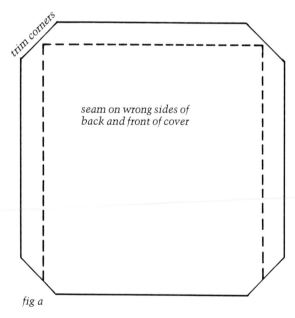

trim corners

seam on wrong sides of back and front of cover

fig a

## Cushion with seed head

The design for this cushion was drawn with a transparent gutta straight on to the stretched silk and left to dry. Then the whole fabric was brushed with thinner. (Some manufacturers recommend water, but use the instructions.) Diagonal stripes were painted on to the wet fabric in different tones (see Watercolour technique).

# Cushions in watercolour technique

The cushion in the foreground includes some resist, or gutta, technique. The tree trunk, branches and a few lines in the foreground have been drawn with transparent gutta. The sky has been painted in light beige and, while this was still wet, the crowns of the trees were painted in brown and copper. When this was dry the middle distance was brushed in with light browns and again left to dry. The sharp contours and highlights were created by plain water brushed on to the dry paints; and, finally, a brush with dark brown paint drew the grasses in the foreground.

The cushion in the centre was also painted in the watercolour technique. This time the stripes run diagonally and the addition of the olive-green and rust colours brightens up the quieter browns.

The cushion in the background was painted with horizontal stripes, wet on wet, in light and dark brown tones. The colours were left to bleed into each other to give a soft and fluid impression without hard contours.

# Light-coloured cushion
*(left)*

The whole silk was dampened with thinner, then colours were painted wet on wet from light beige to mid-brown. When this was dry the trees were painted on with a concentrated black-brown.

# Blue cushion *(middle)*

The whole area was painted with very diluted yellow-orange. When this was dry the contours of the design were drawn with gutta, left to dry again and then coloured in, first the tree trunks with dark brown, then the hills.

Brush and water were used to create highlights. Last, the foliage was painted and sprinkled with salt when still wet.

# Bordeaux coloured cushion *(right)*

A diluted Bordeaux colour was brushed on to the silk as sky, and lines in a deeper tone layered on top as clouds. When this was dry the trees and field were drawn with transparent gutta and, again, left to dry. Then the design was coloured in with diluted as well as more concentrated paints. The field was sprinkled with salt when it was still wet to achieve the textured furrows.

## Foliage and landscape

*(left)*

The main colour of this cushion is grey. The background was painted in the watercolour technique with very soft tones of grey and rose.

The foliage in the foreground was drawn with a dark coloured gutta and, after drying, coloured in with a dark grey.

## Sky landscape cushion

*( top)*

The sky was painted wet on wet and the colours left to run freely into each other. In the middleground the lower edge of the bands of colour were dried quickly with an electric hair-dryer.

The foreground was painted in different browns and, with a clean brush, lines were

This diagram indicates the position of the foreground foliage and distant hills on the cushion shown on the left of page 30.

drawn upwards from the semi-dry edges to give the impression of grasses.

# Blue landscape *(page 30, right)*

Soft tones of grey, blue and turquoise were used for the background. First, the upper part of the landscape was painted and left to dry; then the blue hills were layered over the background. This creates a sharp line, like a row of mountains. The turquoise in the foreground was painted on the still-wet blue. It was left to dry a little and then, with a brush, the grasses were drawn out of the appearing rim around the turquoise patches. The foliage was painted in grey and blue on the dry background. When the foliage was dry plain water was layed over it to create the markings.

## Sky trees and landscape cushion (*top, left*)

First the background was painted with a soft orange and left to dry. Then the design was drawn on with transparent gutta and, again, left to dry.

The landscape was coloured in with brown, orange and olive-green, and the leaves were painted olive-green and a little orange wet on wet. The lines in the foliage were created by letting the paint dry and then adding more wet paint.

## Flower cushion (*centre, below*)

A cushion in watercolour and salt technique. The whole area was painted with thinner; and bands of colour, from soft blue (top) to soft beige (bottom), were painted wet on wet and left to dry. Then concentrated blobs of paint were added for the flowers and the centres immediately sprinkled with salt. When the flowers were dry the salt was brushed off and the stamen and the basket were added in dark brown. When all was dry, the basket weave was painted in with a fine brush and plain water.

## Cushion with hills and trees (*top, right*)

First the whole design was drawn on to the silk with black gutta.

The background was then painted beige, yellow and orange. When the paint was dry water was dripped on to the hill and foliage to create markings. Finally lines were drawn in the foreground with thinner.

## Flower cushion (*left*)

The blossom and leaf motif was drawn with gold gutta (see drawing on page 83). The background is beige and the flowers are Bordeaux and red-brown. The water-lines were drawn from the centre of each flower to give it depth. The leaves were painted in tones of brown and had salt sprinkled on when still wet to provide texture.

## Green cushion (*right*)

After the drawing with gold gutta had dried, the cushion was painted green and salt was sprinkled along the golden branches. The red dots were added last.

## Geese cushion (*above, left*)

A gaggle of geese is marching across this cushion, (see also drawing on page 82). The colours are blue, silver-grey and turquoise. The light blue wing was painted wet on wet with dark blue. The background was also painted in the watercolour technique with tones ranging from silver-grey to blue.

## Blue wall-hanging (*above, top*)

The landscape was drawn with transparent gutta and left to dry. Then it was coloured in with different tones of blue, first very diluted blue for the sky, then hills and houses in stronger colours. After the paints had dried water-lines were painted into the sky and hills.

The crown of the tree was finished last. A few areas were dampened with water, then all was covered with blue, and salt added immediately.

## Cushion with diagonal stripes *(page 34, right)*

Wavy diagonal lines were drawn with transparent gutta. After the whole was dry, the spaces in between the lines were painted in with different greys, rust, yellow and a soft green. Small shapes were left in white as highlights. This design can be used with numerous colour combinations.

## Owl cushion

An owl perches on a pine branch in front of a marbled background. Only a few details are drawn with transparent gutta, 'ears', nose, beak, eyes and some feathers. The rest, including the branch, are painted on to the background and dried immediately with an electric hair-dryer.

## Bird cushion (*left*)

On this cushion the colours are muted. The design (see page 82, top) was drawn with gutta on a soft grey-green background. The bird's beak was painted wet on wet, and the details on its back and on the bark of the branch were brought out with water and a fine brush.

## Bird of Paradise (*right*)

This bird is much more brilliant in colour than the previous subject. The design was drawn with gutta on to a light beige background; then the bird, branch and leaves were painted in yellow, orange, red and different greens.

## Duck cushion (*above*)

The simple contours of the duck and the leaves were drawn in gold gutta. The background was brushed in with a soft lime green, the duck's body with light grey, head rust-red and breast grey-black. Fine brushwork accentuates the plumage.

## Heron cushion (*right*)

This elegant pair of herons was drawn with a dark gutta. For the birds the paint was diluted with water towards the edges and black was added to the wet paint on their tails.

# Silk pictures

Painting on silk is the ideal way of creating an original masterpiece, combining unique shapes and blends of colours. Choose a subject which will add to the atmosphere of a room—strong and bold for a living area; soft and subtle for a bedroom.

When the painting is completed, it will need to be mounted and framed. Most art shops will undertake this whole process for you but if you want to try this stage for yourself, you can also obtain the necessary materials and equipment from the same source.

Compare this picture with the cushion on page 29. For the cushion the same theme, colours and technique were used—a landscape with trees, combining gutta and salt technique to very good effect—yet the final result is quite different. It is true to say that no two silk paintings are ever quite alike. Each one is an original.

# Picture frames

The illustration (Fig a) shows the components that go to make up the mount, back and frame. Either purchase a frame which includes all these accessories, or assemble them separately—old frames can be picked up very cheaply at jumble sales but the backing and mounting materials will need replacing.

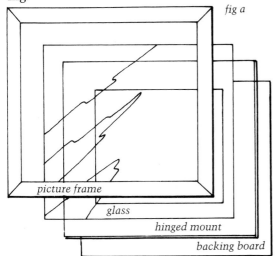

*fig a*

*picture frame*

*glass*

*hinged mount*

*backing board*

## Plain backing

Glazed frames require a firm backing to hold the picture rigid and to keep out dust. The most suitable material is hardboard but some frame mouldings are rather shallow and will not take the thickness of the hardboard. A thin, strong cardboard makes an effective alternative.

## Decorative front mount

The silk painting will not extend to the full area of the material because it had to be pinned out on a frame. The unpainted edges will therefore need to be concealed by a cardboard surround. White, or coloured mounting boards are available at most art shops. Select a colour which will complement the painting, without clashing with the decor of the room.

## Mounting and framing

Cut a piece of decorative mounting card to the inner measurements of the frame and allow an additional ¼in (6mm) all round to fit into the frame rebate. Cut a backing mount to exactly the same size.

Check the area of the painting that needs to be concealed by the decorative mount and pencil in a 'window'. Ensure that this gives a well-balanced sight area of the picture. Use a steel rule and a sharp craft knife to cut out the window, (Fig b).

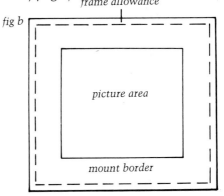

*fig b*

*frame allowance*

*picture area*

*mount border*

To complete the mount, join the top edge of the decorative front and the backing together with strong sticky tape. Position the painting on the backing so that the desired area is seen through the window on the front. Use four strips of double-sided sticky tape to attach the picture to the backing at each corner, (Fig c).

*fig c*

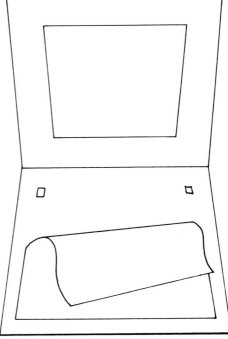

*completed mount*

Place the mounted picture in the frame face downwards. Pin the hardboard back in place with panel pins, lightly tapped into the inner edges of the frame. Attach picture hooks and cord, or picture wire if the frame is heavy.

## Willows in autumn (*above*)

The background of this landscape was painted in watercolour technique. Horizontal stripes were painted on to the wet silk in beige, light and medium browns and a little yellow. When this background was dry a stripe with plain water was drawn across the bottom part of the picture, creating a dark watermark and giving the impression of low hillocks in the

foreground. With a fine brush, vertical lines were drawn out of the watermark to create grasses. All was left to dry completely. Only after this were the willows painted in with thickened paint.

# Willow in summer *(page 40)*

This picture combines watercolour technique and salt technique. The background was painted wet on wet in greens and browns, and while this was still wet, the crowns of the trees were coloured in but the edges of the foliage were dried immediately with an electric hair-dryer. The centres were sprinkled with salt and left to dry slowly. The tree

trunks were painted in last with a fine brush and also dried with a hair-dryer to stop the paint from spreading.

# Landscape with bizarre trees *(above)*

This landscape was painted in watercolour technique with very diluted blue and green. A small amount of Bordeaux colour was added near the horizon and left to dry. The trees were added when the background was completely dry. They were painted with a fine brush and in concentrated colours of brown, blue and red.

## Butterfly

The background was treated with very diluted orange-yellow and left to dry. The contours of the butterfly were drawn (see opposite) with transparent gutta and, again, left to dry. The wings were coloured in with beige, brown, rust and yellow-brown. Some areas were treated with salt when wet, some had water sprinkled on when dry.

The body of the butterfly had water stripes painted in after the background colour had dried a little. Finally the dark brown edge was painted and left to bleed into the pastel coloured background.

# Houses in Denmark

This picture was painted in watercolour technique apart from the door and window frames. To keep these white they were first drawn with gutta and left to dry. The sky was painted with very diluted blue and again left to dry. The roofs of the houses were painted with diluted green and left to dry. Very watery blue and red was used for one house wall, and blue and green for the other. All was left to dry. Spots of water or thinner create the creeper on the wall of the green house.

Diluted green and yellow were applied in the foreground after the houses had dried. Finally the windows were filled with sky-blue and the fences brushed in with dark brown. The distinctive edges around the different colour areas appear when wet paint is applied on a dry background.

# Landscape with tree, in watercolour

The silk was stretched over a frame and brushed all over with thinner (some manufacturers recommend water). Starting at the top of the picture, diluted yellow was painted as far as the horizon in the centre to form the sky. The land was painted from the bottom of the picture to the centre with diluted brown. Broad bands with water or thinner were brushed into the brown area, creating watermarks. These divide the flat brown into a landscape of near and far hills. Some upward brush strokes let grasses grow out of the watermarks.

The tree was painted with concentrated brown and later lightened up with water.

The foliage is a mixture of all the colours used so far. First the colours were left to dry and then, like the trunk lightened with water, they create the watercolour effect.

# Silk scarves

The projects given in this book so far have all had their raw edges concealed by mounting or seaming methods. The edges of a scarf, however, remain visible and they must be finished off very neatly.

A silk scarf with an original design in luminous colours deserves to be finished in the best way. Straight, machine hemming is possible; it is quick but not really worthy of a luxury article. A rolled hem gives the neatest result and can be worked in one of two ways; either by machine and hand, or entirely by machine using a narrow hemmer foot.

## Hand-rolled hem

Make sure all the edges of the silk are perfectly straight. Allow a total of ½in (1cm) around all edges for the finished rolled hem. Work a staystitch with small machine stitches ⅛in (3mm) from the raw edges. Trim the fabric away to within a few threads of the machining. (Fig a).

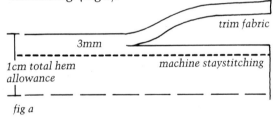

fig a

**Watch point:**
On flimsy fabrics make sure that the machine stitches do not pucker, or snag the material. Use a fine sewing thread, suitable for silk, in a colour to match the edge of the scarf, and a size $^{70}/_{11}$ machine needle. Keep to a stitch tension of about 15–20 stitches per inch.

Turn the full hem allowance to the wrong side and roll the raw edge under so that the line of machine stitching just shows. Thread a fine sewing needle with the same thread and work from right to left along the hem. Sew along the hem with small, loose blind stitches—these are similar to slip-stitches—

working through the machine stitching and the edge of the scarf. Make several stitches and then gently pull up the slack in the thread. This will cause the edge to roll under, (Fig b).

When all the edges have been completed in this way, gently press the centre of the scarf to remove any creases. Do not press the rolled edge, which should be left softly rounded. This is what gives a hand-rolled hem its characteristic appearance.

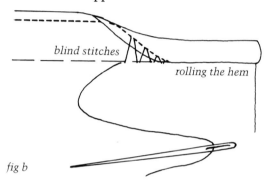

fig b

## Machine-rolled hem

Trim the edge to allow a ¼in (6mm) hem. To hold the hem in place, gently press along the foldline with your fingers. Turn the same edge under again to form a double hem and press with your fingers in the same way.

Slip the double hem into place under the hemmer foot and stitch in place, (Fig c).

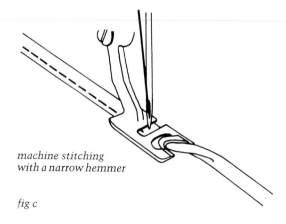

machine stitching
with a narrow hemmer

fig c

## Square scarf with flowers and leaves

This attractive scarf is a good example of the gutta, or resist, technique (see page 14). It shows well the little white blobs, characteristic of this technique, which are created every time a gutta line is started or finished. Only two colours are used—red and grey— but both are shown concentrated and diluted in order to give many tones of red and grey. The red flower dominates the centre while the leaves, mainly in greys and with only a little red, cover the rest of the scarf.

## Blue scarf with yellow-orange blooms

This scarf is painted in gutta, or resist, as well as watercolour technique. First the outlines of the design are drawn with transparent gutta on to the stretched silk and left to dry. Then the background is brushed with slightly diluted dark blue. The same colour as well as more diluted tones of it are used for the leaves.

The flowers are painted in watercolour technique with orange and yellow. The paints are slightly diluted and allowed to flow into each other within the flower petals. It is essential to work quickly before the silk is dry. A band of yellow and orange around the edge of the scarf frames the flower design.

# Scarf with roses

The drawing (on page 83) is enlarged and transferred on to the silk. The outlines, as well as the ribs of the leaves, are drawn with gutta. Soft tones of red and green are painted in and softened further by brushing on clear water whilst the paints are still wet. The stamens are added with concentrated paint when the roses are completely dry. Stripes of soft greens and red are painted along two sides of the scarf to balance the floral design.

# Poppies

The lovely bloom of the poppy provides the inspiration for this scarf. The design is drawn with gold-coloured gutta. The stamens of the open flowers are also kept in gold, which lifts them from the background and adds a lively sparkle to the design. Two sides of the scarf are painted with simple stripes of varying width, repeating the colours of the poppy flowers.

## Scarf painted in three techniques

Three silk-painting techniques – gutta or resist, watercolour and salt technique – are combined in this scarf.

First the stripes around the edges and the outlines of the flowers are drawn in gutta. Two stripes and some of the flowers are painted red-brown, and two further stripes and some details of the flowers are painted black (gutta technique).

The rest of the scarf is painted with a very diluted brown and, whilst the flowers are still wet, their contours and details are added in a reddish-brown (watercolour technique).

Some of the leaves are sprinkled with salt whilst the silk is still wet, in order to create a lively marbled effect (salt technique).

When working in watercolour or salt one has to paint quite fast, as the whole design needs to be finished while the silk is still wet.

## Detail of a scarf of crepe georgette

The picture shows a detail of a mountainous landscape with a farmhouse (see page 84). It is painted on a very fine and transparent crepe georgette. The design is first drawn with gutta, left to dry, and then coloured in. The only colours used are brown and red mixed in different proportions and sometimes diluted with water.

# Scarf with yellow flowers

This design provides very good practice at drawing flowing lines with gutta. Leaves, petals and stripes are painted in different tones of yellow and grey. The stamens, finally, are added with a fine brush and concentrated paint after the background is dry.

# Scarf with alpine flowers

A walk in the Alps gave the idea for this design, a naturalistic drawing of delicate alpine flowers balanced by very strong geometric bands on the two opposite sides in the same colours. The flowers in the foreground are painted in strong tones; the flowers, leaves and grasses further back are watered down to make them softer. The blooms of the gentian and the silver thistle are painted in watercolour technique to give them more detail and depth. The rest was painted in the simpler gutta, or resist technique.

## Magnolia scarf

This scarf shows a similar arrangement to the poppies one on page 50, but through the softer nature of the blossom, and the gentler colour scheme, the overall impression is quite different. Again the design is drawn with gutta, the blossom is painted in water-colour technique with rose, brown and a little grey. The coloured stripes are just mixtures of rose and brown, concentrated or diluted.

# Peacock feather design

The elegant design of a peacock's feather is drawn on to the silk with gutta and left to dry (see page 84). The swirling lines of the feather are particularly suitable for the gutta, or resist technique as gutta is easiest to apply in continuous flowing lines.

## Scarf in red and blue

The whole scarf was worked in the gutta, or resist method, using transparent gutta, red and blue paints, and mixtures of these. Colours from the same manufacturer can be mixed, but it is not advisable to mix paints of different makes.

## Abstract scarf

Here, as a contrast to the previous naturalistic designs, is a completely abstract drawing with very fine lines but a strict, con-
trolled colour scheme. The warm tones pre-
dominate.

Working outwards from one corner of the
scarf, the random shapes are drawn in with
transparent gutta. Within these outlines, soft
beige, pink, coral and red hues are applied and
layered in the watercolour technique, to
create a warm and glowing effect.

## Alphabet squares

Letters in many different shapes and sizes are the only design element in this attractive scarf. They are arranged in a two-dimensional pattern drawn with transparent gutta. Drawing straight lines with a resist agent requires a very steady hand and quick work.

The imaginative colour scheme not only brings this design to life but also offers good practice in colour mixing (see page 11).

## Rose and beige flower scarf

This delicate design makes use of very fine gutta lines and large areas of soft, pale water-colours.

The stylized blooms and leaves are painted in shades of soft rose, grey and beige and the centre of the scarf is left in white. The whole scarf is edged with two narrow borders of rose and a wide border of beige.

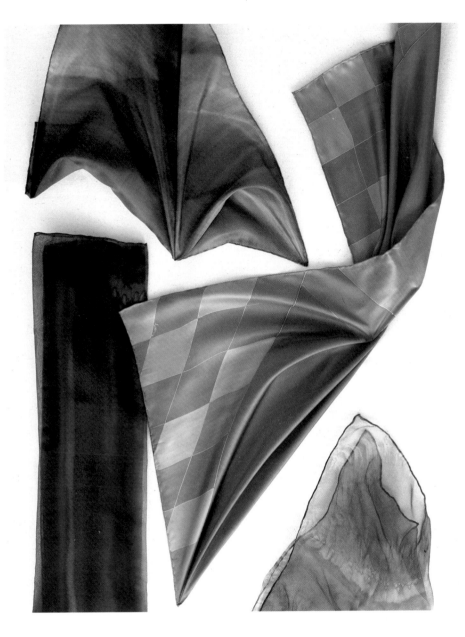

## Four scarves

This selection of four scarves illustrates the use of simple gutta, or resist, and watercolour techniques on different fabrics. The materials used range from fine silk chiffon, with a matt appearance, to heavier weights of shiny silk. Each example shows the choice of warm, bold colours to perfect effect.

The scarves do not have to be square in shape and long, rectangular ones have a variety of uses as fashion accessories.

# Fashion

When you make a garment from pure silk that has also been hand-painted, you are entering the world of haute couture. Having perfected your skill at painting on silk, you must also have some basic knowledge of dressmaking to undertake the projects shown in this section. The following hints will also be useful in producing perfect results.

Delicate fabrics need careful treatment to obtain the best results, so use fine pins, needles and thread, and special finishes for seams and hems.

Try not to handle the material too much and keep the number of rows of machining to an absolute minimum—this avoids the risk of marking or puckering the fabric.

The choice of style for a silk garment is of prime importance. It should be soft and flowing, with gathers and unpressed pleats, rather than a figure-hugging shape. Select patterns with the minimum of seaming and try to avoid those which require facings, as these will show through as ridges on the garment.

Seams and hems must not be too bulky. An overedge seam is the simplest method but care must be taken not to work the zigzag stitches too tightly, or the seam will be drawn up and the garment will not hang correctly. Use a mock French seam in place of the normal version, as this is easier to control when machining round curves. There is also less risk of puckering the fabric with this method, as the first stage produces the seam that shows on the right side of the garment. A self-bound seam gives a very neat finish and is suitable for straight or curved seams.

Silk with its luxurious softness and sheen has always been a favourite in high fashion. Now it is up to you to combine the fabric with stunning designs and daring colour schemes to create original garments of striking elegance! Choose a dress of simple cut which will show your painting to its best advantage. Make sure that the design fits well into the shape of the individual garment pieces. It may help to have the outlines of the garment pieces marked on the silk with a soft pencil before starting to paint, but do not forget: that an initial seam allowance is needed of at least ½in (1cm).

## Overedge seam

With the right sides of the pieces facing each other, machine along the seamline. Gently press both seam allowances flat towards the back of the garment. Trim both allowances to ¼in (6mm).

Use close, short machine zigzag stitches to join the raw edges together, or overcast the edges by hand, (Fig a).

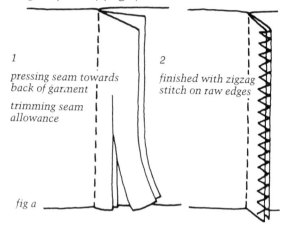

*1*
*pressing seam towards back of garment*

*trimming seam allowance*

*2*
*finished with zigzag stitch on raw edges*

*fig a*

## Mock French seam

With the right sides of the pieces facing each other, machine along the seamline. Gently press both seam allowances flat towards the back of the garment.

Fold the raw edges of both pieces ⅛in (3mm) in to face each other. Finger press together, (see page 46), and pin close to the folded edges. Machine along this edge to complete the seam, (Fig b).

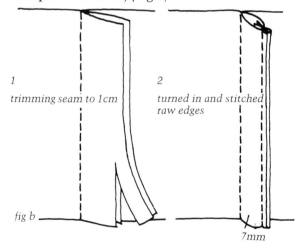

*1*
*trimming seam to 1cm*

*2*
*turned in and stitched raw edges*

*fig b*

*7mm*

## Self-bound seam

With the right sides of the pieces facing each other, machine along the seamline. Gently press both seam allowances flat towards the back of the garment. Trim the seam allowance closest to the garment to ⅛in (3mm), and use the other allowance to bind them both together.

Turn under ⅛in (3mm) of the untrimmed seam allowance to the seamline, enclosing the trimmed edge. Machine stitch or hand sew, keeping just above the previous line of machining, (Fig c).

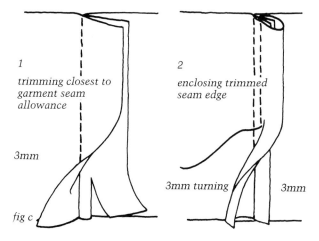

*1*
*trimming closest to garment seam allowance*

*3mm*

*fig c*

*2*
*enclosing trimmed seam edge*

*3mm turning*     *3mm*

## Evening dress of crepe-de-chine

The glowing silk colours are used undiluted and in a striking combination.

The large-scale design of stylized flowers and swirling garlands is drawn with transparent gutta on to a natural coloured silk. Then the design is coloured in with red and turquoise. Finally the background is painted with a deep green. The design goes well with the simple cut of the garment. It emphasizes the neckline and shoulders, divides the skirt into large panels, and decorates the hemline.

# Evening dress with butterfly stole in crepe-de-chine

The very straight cut of this dress is under-lined by the plain striped pattern drawn with gold gutta and painted in blue green and turquoise. In strong contrast the soft falling butterfly stole is decorated in lively flowing lines and painted in the same undiluted col-ours as the dress. The movement of the stole in contrast with the calm of the dress gives this garment a very special charm.

## Loose-fitting blouse in crepe-de-chine

Uncomplicated cuts are more suitable for garments made of hand-painted silk as they show the designs and colour schemes to their best advantage. This is demonstrated with this wide-cut blouse, where even the sleeve is included in the design without interruption. The undiluted colours of yellow and orange give a very summery impression, slightly softened with a diluted bordeaux.

## Quilted jacket in gutta technique

For this jacket with raglan sleeves the design of overlapping leaves is kept to the main areas of the garment pattern pieces, back, sleeve and collar, so that it will not interfere with the making up of the jacket.

The design is drawn in transparent gutta on to natural coloured silk, coloured in with undiluted deep green and turquoise. The background is painted with a diluted blue. The jacket is lined with a dark blue silk and interlined with synthetic wadding.

Before the garment is made up, the back, sleeves and collar are machine-quilted along the lines of the leaf design.

In the background a silk picture is visible of farm buildings in the watercolour technique.

# Wadded jacket

The fabric again is painted in the gutta technique, and the design is kept to the main panels of the garment pattern. Note how the design is adapted so as not to interfere with the centre back seam of the collar or the seams of the raglan sleeves. The colours used are slightly diluted brown and olive-green and a concentrated orange.

*Enlarge this drawing to the size required to fit into the area of fabric on the back of the jacket. You can add further gutta lines by hand to complete the design.*

## Blouse and matching sleeveless jacket

Two different kinds of silk are used for this outfit, but painted in the same colours. The blouse is made of crepe-de-chine, and the sleeveless jacket of silk taffeta. These garments show how effective a very simple arrangement of stripes can be. A flair with colours can be more important than any drawing skill. Concentrated olive-green is combined with undiluted blue and a small amount of concentrated warm orange.

Where the colours lay side by side on the same piece of fabric they are divided by the fine white line left by the gutta, but where they come together at a seam no gutta line is needed. Note the centre seam on the blouse sleeve.

# Blouse with dolman sleeves

This soft, crepe-de-chine blouse is a very simple shape and as it only requires two pieces, it is the ideal choice for an inexperienced dressmaker. The sleeves are cut in one with the body, see page 75 for the pattern diagram.

**Watch point:**
Crepe-de-chine absorbs a lot of dye, so make sure you mix a sufficient quantity before beginning to paint.

The geometric patterns across the yoke and shoulders are drawn in with transparent gutta on the back and front. A similar motif is drawn from the hemline to a point on the left-hand side of the front.

These geometric patterns call for very straight gutta lines. Even people with a steady hand may feel happier using a large ruler to apply the gutta.

## Headband, blouse, trousers and skirt

Headband and skirt are made from a very fine muslin silk and painted with cyclamen and red diluted to varying degrees. Blouse and trousers are made from twill silk. The design of the blouse was drawn with black gutta and painted with red and yellow mixed as well as cyclamen.

The background of the blouse and the trousers is painted with a sponge, which is useful for working as fast as possible to prevent uneven colouring. (Remember to protect your hands when using a sponge.)

# Wrapped trousers

For these trousers it is essential that the shape of the trouser pattern is drawn on to the fabric. After this is done, colour the pattern parts red to within 2in (5cm) of the seam-line.

Leave it to dry. When the red paint is completely dry, paint the last 2in (5cm) around the edge of the trousers yellow. Since no gutta has been used the yellow will create a zigzag line where it flows into the red.

## Waistcoat with flowers

This waistcoat with a dark blue background has a floral painted border. Alcohol-based paints are used and black gutta. Afterwards plain alcohol is brushed over the design. This softens the colours and blurs the edges. Water-based paint gives the same effect when clean water is brushed over a design.

## Chemise

The shape of this elegant chemise and the simple motif, make it the ideal choice for your first venture into the field of fashion, as it requires the minimum of painting and dress-making skills.

On a natural cream background, draw basic blossom shapes on the front and back sections of the chemise with colourless gutta. When the gutta has completely dried, colour the whole surface of the fabric, using a sponge to apply the paint evenly.

## Short-sleeved blouse

This striking blouse has short sleeves, cut in one with the body, and a slashed neckline. It is a simple shape, suitable for an inexperienced needlewoman.

The front of the blouse shows a stylized Chinese blossom and butterfly design, worked in gutta and watercolour techniques. Shades of pink, orange and Bordeaux are set against a bold tangerine background.

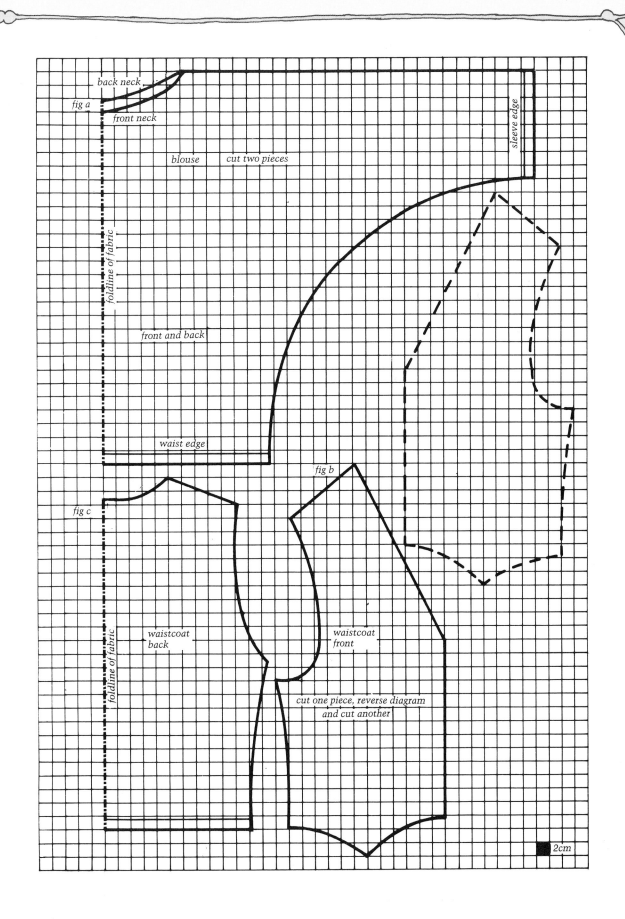

back neck

fig a

front neck

blouse    cut two pieces

sleeve edge

foldline of fabric

front and back

waist edge

fig b

fig c

foldline of fabric

waistcoat
back

waistcoat
front

cut one piece, reverse diagram
and cut another

2cm

# Other ideas

Silk paints applied and fixed as recommended by the manufacturers are colourfast for dry-cleaning and handwashing. This means it is possible to decorate a large variety of household goods and furnishings. These include table cloths, curtains, lampshades, screens and room dividers, but you will find many other suitable outlets for your new skill.

The inexperienced painter, however, should start with a smaller article. For example, a lampshade offers plenty of scope from the design point of view. Choose a simple, coolie-hat shape for your first venture, (see page 80).

## Selecting a frame

Most lampshade frames are made of copper wire but white, plastic-covered frames are also readily available. As these are rustproof, they save time in preparing the frame. New frames can be purchased in handicraft shops but you can find interesting old frames in junk shops, or at jumble sales, which you can easily re-cover.

A fabric shade which has been mounted on to card only needs a frame at the top and the bottom, but fabric which is not mounted requires a strutted frame, where the top and bottom rings are held in place by side struts.

## Binding a frame

Copper-wire frames must be bound with tape to prevent them marking the covering material. A ½in (1cm) wide soft, straight tape is the most suitable material. Measure all the struts and the circumferences of the rings of the frame and allow about two and a quarter times this total length in tape.

If the frame is strutted, bind these first. Fold about 1in (2.5cm) over the top ring and down on to the strut, (Fig a). Wind the tape

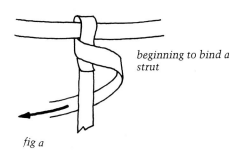

*beginning to bind a strut*

*fig a*

diagonally round the strut and cover the starting end. Continue down the strut, pulling the tape very taut. When you have reached the other end of the strut, take the tape behind the bound strut, over the ring and then under itself again. Pull the knot tight, (Fig b). Bind all the remaining struts, except one, in this way.

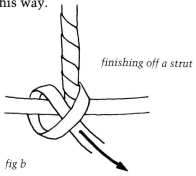

*finishing off a strut*

*fig b*

Bind the top ring, beginning at the top of the unbound strut. Work all the way round, binding in a figure of eight where the struts join the ring, (Fig c). Work down the remaining strut, then round the bottom ring. To finish off, turn under ¼in (6mm) at the end of the tape and stitch neatly to the wrapped tape on the inside of the ring.

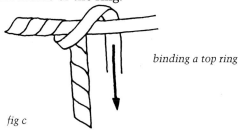

*binding a top ring*

*fig c*

## Making the shade

Clearly mark the shape of the shade, plus ¾in (2cm) seam allowance, on the silk. Paint the silk as usual, fitting the design into the shape of the shade but also colouring the marked seam allowance.

**Watch point:**
It is particularly important that silk paints are properly fixed when making a lampshade, as the silk is exposed to intensive light and heat every time the lamp is switched on.

Working on a clean, dry surface – such as a formica-topped table – and using double-sided sticky tape, stick the silk face down on to the tape. It should be well stretched but not distorted. This holds the fabric taut ready to commence the next stage.

Cut the shape of the lampshade from a self-adhesive lampshade card, (Fig d), and stick it to the wrong side of the silk, leaving an even seam allowance of ¾in (2cm) all the way round. Try to avoid any puckering or air bubbles. Cut along the cutting lines marked on the silk.

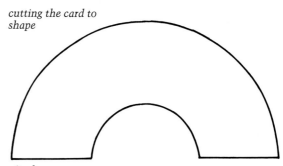

*cutting the card to shape*

*fig d*

Fit the stiffened shade around the frame and stitch down the side seam with adhesive. Fold the seam allowance at the top and bottom over the frame and stick it to the inside of the frame.

## Tablecloths

A table cloth may be painted to be the perfect match for your dinner service, with patterns and colours taken from the china or crockery.

Table cloths in complicated shapes or very large ones may be painted in manageable squares and fitted or joined after fixing.

## Screen in Honan silk

This ambitious screen, or room divider, demonstrates that not only scarves and cushions may be decorated with silk paints. The wooden framework is simple enough to be made by any 'do-it-yourself' woodworker. The silk panels are stuck on with double-sided sellotape.

The stylized flower motif is repeated on each of the three panels with slight variations. It is worked in the gutta technique (page 14). The only colours used are different warm tones of brown, from a soft ochre to deep brown.

# Room divider

The frame for this room divider has been made up from tubular steel rods and has been fitted with casters.

Work a hem at the top and bottom of each silk panel to fit over the top and bottom rails of the steel frame, or stick the silk to the frame with double-sided sellotape.

# Lampshade

The lower half of this lampshade is decorated in the salt technique. The feathery leaves on the upper half are painted in with black on the salmon-coloured dry background.

# Motifs for
# silk painting

ABCDEF

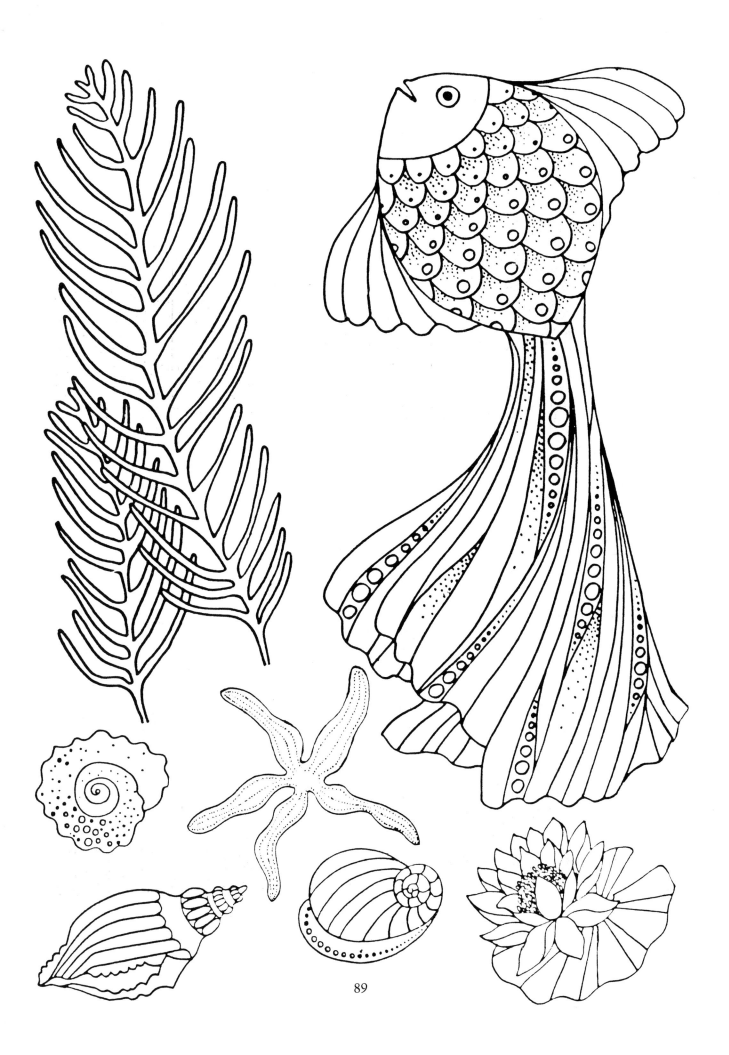

94

95

# INDEX

*If readers have difficulty obtaining any of the materials or equipment mentioned in this book, please write for further information to the publishers, Search Press Ltd., Wellwood, North Farm Road, Tunbridge Wells, Kent TN2 3DR, England*

**If you are interested in any other of the art and craft titles published by Search Press please send for free colour catalogue to:**
Search Press Ltd, Dept B, Wellwood, North Farm Road, Tunbridge Wells, Kent TN2 3DR.